TOWARDS THE HORIZON

By the same author:
Through The Window (2007)

TOWARDS THE HORIZON

J.R. Ashley

Book Guild Publishing
Sussex, England

First published in Great Britain in 2015 by
The Book Guild Ltd
The Werks
45 Church Road
Hove, BN3 2BE

Typesetting in Bembo by
Ellipsis Digital Ltd, Glasgow

Printed in Great Britain by
CPI Group (UK) Ltd, Croydon, CR0 4YY

A catalogue record for this book is available from
The British Library.

ISBN 978 1 910298 17 6

I see better when my eyes are shut, when everyday matters become less dominant.

CONTENTS

Acknowledgements

I would like to thank my friends Margaret Broadhurst, Frank Blamey, Alan Taylor, without whose help and patience I would never have been able to proceed.

MOOD RAKER

To you and me the weather is benign;
The long and lazy summer days stretch
The boundaries of the imagination to the full,
Like the blue horizon rolls on to accommodate
Uninterrupted golden wheat field prairies.

But not so to him.

The sun lies deep within dark thunder clouds;
Heavy rain blasts down on roof and on garden path,
Rattling like nails thrust from an exploding bomb.
He sits in his rocking chair and waits,
The storm shakes the foundation of his being.

But tomorrow, when he basks in bright sunshine,
Where will we be?

SCHOLAR'S REACH

When the outflowing tide has satisfied its thirst
And drunk the waters from the upper reach,
When river flies swarmed and turned to chase
The same retreading tide exposing the sandbank,
Everything has gone, the area is drained
From fulfilment, meaningfully to starting point.

Like late evening before night time arrives,
The light having withered, shrinking into a hidden place;
Like autumn's vanquished maturity retreats leaving
A hollow hiatus before the start of winter;
Like the mould of leaves in the poet's world
Waiting for the brave snowdrops to appear.

He shuffles his ruffle of papers into a pile
As if he were shovelling stone into a gravel pit,
He did not hear or heed the consequential sound
Reverberate through the examination hall:
He was finished, three years of hard study work
Had gushed out the opening in his mind.

Exhausted, bare, nothing there, nothing left,
An emptiness within a body aware of a heartbeat
With no response except for consciousness of breathing
Outside the reality of being;
A mental vacuum waiting for the tide to turn
And refill all that vacated space.

WONDERFUL WORLD

Before I die,
I would like to see again
The glowing sky at sunset,
And count the bees
In the apple blossom.

I would like to climb the hill,
Look down and identify once more

The oak tree and the ash,
The beech tree and the sycamore
In the rich wild wood below.

I would like to witness swallows
Gathering on the pylon lines,
And refamiliarise myself
With gaudy celandines
And drifts of bluebells and anemones.

But I do not bemoan my blindness,
Berate the fate that caught me in its web;
Many pleasures there undoubtedly were
Which now elude me,
But there is much to compensate.

The whoosh and bark of wild geese on the wing,
The quietness as the blackbird sings,
The beckoning of the tired face
Refreshed by the breeze coming from the sea,
After a long hot day.

The heightened sense of change of season,
The swings of moods in people's company,
The anonymity of oneself
Over long periods of time,
And the reciprocating touch of someone close.

SILENT WITNESS

The mirror bowed its head in shame.
'But I was not to blame,' it said,
'I only saw and kept my counsel.'

CIVIC DECEPTION

There is a breed amongst us,
Through lack of intelligence
Steers its ship through deep waters
By shallow eloquence.

And in so doing
By its own volition
Identifies itself
As a politician.

THE TEMPO OF THE DANCE

Quick!
Quick!
Focus attention
And attune to the situation.

Quick!
The hare bobs up from the bracken,
The otter's snout appears for a second
Above the surface of the brook.

Quick!
The sleight of the magician's hand,
The lightning flashing
Through the darkness.

Slow!
The patient unable to move,
Using surrounding walls as tapestry
On which to weave circuitous imaginings.

Slow!
The sun taking its time
To pierce the trees in the forest glade
Or disperse midwinter frost.

Slow, slow!
The owl choosing his moment
To silently sweep
Across the cobbled yard.

FISHING

'Bliss! Bliss! What perfect bliss,'
The poet said, chucking his pens away
To go on one week's holiday,
And dig for worms, and fish and fish.
'What bliss, what perfect unalloyed bliss.'

THE IMPORTANCE OF TIME

Play the tune in June;
It's not the same in December.
For life and living are based on time,
And timing is everything.

THE MAN WITH A PROBLEM

He functions in the quotas of extremes,
No in betweens, no degrees of shade.
He is absolutely 'for' or 'against',
He is wholly with or wholly without,
He is the basic raw machine
That's switched full 'on' or 'off'.

Happiness to bleak despair,
Generosity to meanness
That turns a prize of gold to dust,
Leadership with flags aflying
To hermit sitting in his cave,
Eyes transfixed on dripping walls.

The will to listen isn't there,
Nor the power to mediate alternatives;
Consideration is synonymous with dalliance,
Comfort is in the certainty
Of definite colours, black or white,
No recognition of the fertile land between.

THE GARDEN SHED

In summer storm no greater thrill
Than sheltering in the garden shed
Amongst dryness and dust,

Lawnmower smells and scraps of oily rag,
Evoking times of days long gone,
Bowls, open French windows, picnic teas.

Days when Father could do anything,
Like mend my bike or build a pond,
And Mother made raspberry jam
From fruit we freshly picked.
But neither of them conspicuously there
To restrain my play of innocence.

And running the dog in Vale Royal woods
And damming the stream till it overflowed,
And counting the eggs in the thrush's nest
When she wasn't there.
Times when if an aeroplane flew above,
Everything stopped as we searched the sky.

How odd that rain on the old shed roof
Should bring back memories of my youth,
When sunshine was predominantly
The order of the day.

GENETICALLY MODIFIED

In this country
Every possible two steps forward
Promotes a cautious one step back.
Hoards of the feeble
Pester me
With this philosophy.

Come!
Leave behind the reactionaries,
If they haven't got the courage,
The foresight to allow the experiments,
They deserve to starve and rot –
The stupid lot.

HEARTBREAK HILL

The floor is the fallen leaves of oak
In the stubble at the cornfield's edge,
The ceiling the evening sky.
Entanglements of bramble climb through
The ruins of the red brick barn,
The frameless window gives a distant view.

The chemistry of autumn
Is here in one place,
In one field, in one space,
Squeezing this late season
Into tinctures of memory
Of the two of us.

The memory drips like anaesthetic
Creating a numbed void in me.
A void that was to follow
The opening of the cornfield gate
Onto the track that leads
To Heartbreak Hill.

MIRROR ON THE WALL

Is it him, the man I knew?
He looks the same, but a little older,
His enquiring eyes seem less bright
And his voice of command a faint echo,
A mutter enquiring of and to himself.

His name is the same, and where he lives,
The left-hand side of 'Crowsnest Lane',
Familiar curtains and ornaments
Adorn his room, and there is his armchair
Which once was surrounded by books piled high.

Is it him, the man I had known?
Surely not. His persona hangs
Like a dull wet overcoat.
Unsure I look again and turn away:
The man I had seen was no longer there.

NONCONFORMITY

Seldom do we find a fence in a forest,
Peanuts in porridge,
Pears in an apple orchard,
Or publicans tortured
With thirst.

Seldom, a rabbit in a city street,
A pensive moon through sleet,
Pleasure in pain,
Children dancing in rain
In winter cold.

When we do, such things provide
A focal point, a rare divide:
To peaceful minds, an interruption;
A surprise disruption
To conformity.

To the young an inspiration, excitement,
A chance declaration of vagaries ahead;
To us older folk a jolt,
A setback from what we had known
And what we had seen or expected.

THE EASY PATH

My mind says
That reluctant acceptance
Is deceit,
For although it may at first
Weigh in the positive balance,
In the end it is less
Than having weighed nothing at all.

It has negative potential;
It puts an unreliable rung
In the ladder
On the way to the stars.
It pretends responsibility;
In victory it claims unwarranted glory,
Absolves itself in defeat.

Its door is wide open
And I mistakenly walk in.

NOVEMBER DAWN

It starts to be seen faintly after six o'clock,
A thin white pencil line where field meets sky.
To unfamiliar eyes this may seem
To be a solid bank of threatening cloud.

No movement in nature, nor any natural sounds,
No song of birds, no welcoming fanfare;
Only the noise of a distant motor car
Early to avoid the city rush.

Any stars that might have been have gone,
And, but for my breathing the air seems not to exist,
Neither warm nor cold, a sense of neutrality
Occupies the space between me and the world.

The thin line is reluctant to break and spread,
As if its energy is already spent,
A dire forecast of the positive certainty
Of the uncertainty of the day ahead.

GROWING DOWN

On the way down from high horse
To being knocked flat, like a fish,
I pause in the field of short grass,
Not boring bowling green grass,
But grass nibbled by rabbits,
I tell myself how useless high horse was.

I pause and reflect
That the growing-up had been hurried,
A willowy nondescript adolescence
Of innocence, virginity and silly wonderment,
A game of 'Guess who's tallest,
You or me!'

Growing down is searching, finding,
Winding through bypassed dominions
Unexplored in the chase to reach the moon,
Or trodden on and then dismissed;
For here it will be found that maturity
Lies in not accepting but understanding.

THE HUMAN FACTOR

In the order of being,
Are we any more
Than a grain of salt,
A blot of ink,
A wind-blown leaf?

Perhaps we are,
Especially when
We strut our stuff to others,
Reflecting in the glories
That just happen to be about.

This is transient though,
Even reflects dependency on others
To boost our ego.
What have we really done
To warrant this self-esteem?

Perhaps we've changed habits and fashions;
We now take longer than we did
To become old, and to die,

We've integrated society,
Coded education, law and order.

Art has been progressed
From portraits and landscapes
To unmade beds,
Piles of bricks
And canvases washed with colour.

In science,
We go on knowing more and more,
The moon has been reached and walked upon,
We consider ourselves more advanced
Than any other generation.

I wonder why the cat sits and smiles?

THE LIGHT

The light lingers
Like the last person in the bar,
Then it goes off and we panic
And rush to see why.
We then realise
That the only time we notice it being on,
Is when it's off.

FLIES

When flies fly high
Into the sky
And we are bound
Flat-footed to the ground,
Why do we then, when underground,
Spring wings and sing
'Hallelujah to the King'?

HIGH HOPES MANOR

Fred was thinking of a bright new car
As he followed me through the gate,
And Maud the spangled party dress
She was to buy for daughter Kate.

Joe was planning a holiday
To India or maybe Tibet,
And pondering who to take with him,
Gladys or Yvette.

Then, the 'God-Almighty' crash:
For all their hopes were built
On the now vacated mansion house,
I had mortgaged to the hilt.

WORLD WITHOUT WORDS

Picture punctuation
Without accompanying words,
And you have me in your sights;
Questions, exclamations,
And pauses of varying lengths.
No need for Fowler
Or the *Oxford English Dictionary*
Nor Roget and his thesaurus.
Not being tongued-tied, I'd be free
Of rhythms, idioms and rhymes,
I would loosen my tie and be
A relaxed person again.

No Ps and Qs to mind,
No words of explanation,
No qualifying phrase to cover
The threat of disclamation.
What a peaceful life it would be,
No falling out, one with another,
No cursing of the cat,
Obscenities kept undercover.
Only a quiet calmness,
Tranquil with song of birds
The rustles of leaves on trees
And the flowing brook.

RUSTIC SWEETHEARTS

I is a country yokel,
And I use words
As I find 'em.

'Ye are' sounds like
A police car
Disappearin' out of sight.

But be it as it may
'Ye are' (or is it 'you is')
The one I loves.

And you loves I,
And we are committed
One t'each other, like.

BLINDNESS

Like the deaf person can hear
The silent strains of the symphony,
So the blind man sees
The innuendo that exudes
Into the atmosphere
When a crowd is congregate
And he is amongst it,
But separate.

He sees the smiles, the admiration,
The openness, the caution of one to another,
The smirks, the envy, the greed,
The politics and its disputes.
He wonders where and on whose side
He would comfortably sit,
But he is fully aware
That he's no longer a positive part of it.

THE FLY

When and where I am wondering why,
I go to town on the back of a fly,
And on the way home I drop from the sky
And fall into a treacle pie.

Sigh, sigh, why oh why,
I had to land in a treacle pie,
When all the time within my heart
There's longing for an apple tart.

CHRISTMAS

Christmas is for children,
The very young, unquestioning belief
In what they see and what they hear,
In Santa Claus and all he brings
In reindeer, rooftops and chimneys swept,
In glister tinsel and Christmas trees
Decorated distinctively with fairy lights.

And later, still believing,
The day is filled with toys and games
And picture books and things to eat;
Never before such freedom of choice,
Laughter, running, pushing, rolling,
Snatching, throwing and ending up
With broken pieces and in tears.

And later still when the secret,
The bitter pill, is coated with the fact
Of sharing 'the knowledge' with bigger boys,
There are bicycles and books and championships
And planning what to do in the holidays;
And more, that token of growing up,
The keeping of pretence to the younger ones.

And so the progress to parenthood,
When we start to reminisce,
Recalling snow up to the window ledge,
Snow just right to make snowballs and a snowman,
Sliding and skating on the frozen pond;
Red scarves, red hat, and a small red robin
Watching from the snow-covered stump.

But Granddad ponders, 'A likely tale,
Was it ever really like that on Christmas Day?'
He looks out from the centrally heated room
At the grass on the lawn which has started to grow,
Daffodil and crocus shoots have started to show
And the ducks on the pond are livening up,
All in the glow of the late afternoon sunshine.

ROUND THE CORNER

What is round the corner?
I always wish to see,
But if I ever get there,
Another there's bound to be.

But I am so determined,
It is my one intent,
And I know that if I get there
It will be with God's consent.

For life is all a mystery
From beginning to the end;
We search, and seeing, find not.
Who am I to comprehend?

HERD INSTINCT

If follows
That when two people meet,
Or ten or twenty,
Their individual personality shifts.

Quiet reserve turns to truculence,
Enquiry to inquisition,
Friendly play to riotous behaviour;
All these can happen.

Wealth and poverty,
Dominance and servility,
Adjust to circumstance,
Assume subtle transformation.

The bringing together of people
Awakes a stark awareness of oneself,
The showing of strength,
The hiding of inadequacy.

The syndrome is of leader and the led,
A contest of minds
And the shuttlecocking of bodies
Into a pecking order.

INSUBSTANTIAL EVIDENCE

A lonely desolate spot,
Even on a bright summer's day,
But the light had gone by half past three
And it is night now, in late November.
The lean trees howling in the wind
Give no protection to the house.

Moon: a momentary glimpse
Of attic windows and gable ends,
Of stable, and of stable yard.
An obscure mystery shadow creeps
By thicket hedge and across the lawn,
Then darkness once again.

‘Why keep on living here?’
Agnes had asked in her usual way.
‘I’ll see you tomorrow, keep the door locked
And don’t lift the safety-chain for anyone.’
She mounted her machine and went down the drive:
I watched her tail light disappear.

Room Victorian,
Artificially warmed with clutter and must,
With dust in high places
And dying embers in the hearth
Near where I sit and wait and stare and think:
Locked doors will not keep him away.

Sound, the smallest shift,
Be it a mouse in the wainscot
Or movement of weights in the grandfather clock,
Unravelling the equilibrium of sense
That linked the body to the mind to the soul.
Then the hall door opened.

Silence; no one spoke,
But he let me recognise his face.
The knife moved clean and straight for the heart;
Warm blood trickled down my shirt.
The wound-up clockwork spring of life had snapped,
And I was dying, dead.

With morning came flurries of action, and words:
‘He hadn’t seemed very well all day,’ she said calmly.
‘Well, there’s no sign of suffering,
It was probably a heart attack,’ he said.

'But what about the wound and the blood?'
I said, but no one heard.

The wind continued to blow,
Rattling the windows,
Searching, searching.

MONDAY MORNING

Monday morning will come,
Whether it be Tuesday,
Friday, Sunday night
Or somewhere in between:
Monday morning will come.

It will surely come,
As blood spurts from a naked wound,
And hounds will chase the fox's scent,
As mirrors reflect the truth
And lovers will quarrel.

Yes, it will come,
Like rain from heavy clouds
Or warmth from the afternoon sun,
Like vile vapour from the heap of dung
Or sweet fragrance from hawthorn blossom.

And when it comes, then it will bring
Routine back to the workaday life;
The clock will restart to tell the time anew
And a tiny fragment of the mind
Will exclaim: here we go again.

SOLITUDE

No noise this night;
The sound of silence
Observes no obstruction.
It creeps under a door
Or through a crack in a window.
It smothers the hills
And rolls down into the valley
To where the lake lies still.

The heavy darkness
Presses the sky down
To below the tops of trees,
Bringing silence and stillness
Within the reach
Of the human mind,
Compressing its tentacles
One into another.

With no distraction
From daylight and noise,
From moving things
And other human beings
Competing for space,
I am left
In my rocking chair
Inviolate.

Inviolate!
From what,
A kingdom commanding
An empty box,
Darkness no light,
Quietness no noise,
Stillness no movement,
What world am I in?

VACANCIES

Politicians have the most difficult job,
But because their aspirations and gift of the gob
Exceed their intelligence,
They quickly become unfit for purpose,
And surplus.

WHAT WILL BE . . .

What is the end at the end of the road
When the grass verge peters away?
When the horizon rushes to greet us
Is there a vision beyond?

Life being a series of episodes
Does not prepare us for this;
Ends herald the beginnings
In continuity.

So used we are, to day following night
And summer the winter and spring;
So used to sunshine after rain
And following morning dew.

When the clock stops, when the chain snaps,
It is impossible to think
What the end is at the end of the road,
Where the grass verge peters out.

WAITING

I linger long,
For lingering brings
Vestige of hope
To fading things.

Like being a part
Of the TV millions
Watching the rain
On the cricket pavilion.

Like waiting for the postman
When he has been and gone,
Thinking he might return
With the important one.

FAMILY PICTURE GALLERY

The future is the 'will be'
Not quite to hand,
To be lived for,
To be lived with
Tomorrow.

Today is the future of
Yesterday:
Today bears the fruit
That sets the seed
For tomorrow.

It is the nature of life
That death will come:
But some vital part will persist,
Leaving a grain
That can be built upon.

We review the pictures on the wall;
We filter them
Into our own personality,
Carrying them into the uncertain
Certainty of the future.

And later on, when you and I are gone,
Perhaps an image hanging dustily

In some secluded place,
Some descendant, unawares,
Will affect a familiar mannerism.

They may ponder for a while
Not recognising the situation,
Ponder again,
Wondering what they have seen
And then understand.

DESPAIR

If everything is ours
Like the sun and the showers –
If we share all that's in life,
The love and the strife –
Then why does it all
Appal?

LONELINESS

Despite everything
It comes over one,
A feeling of loneliness.

At first, dare I say,
It comes deceitfully,
As if it wasn't there.

It creeps, as if natural,
Like dusk in the hedgerows
Before the onset of night.

Then suddenly
One becomes aware
Of a confining nothingness.

Much like
Being locked in an iron cage
Without the key.

Captive of recurring memories;
Oh, let them be gone,
Melancholy is hindrance to the future.

Thank God
Somewhere inside
A light begins to glimmer.

LOVE PAINS

Stab yourself with the end of a stake
Or on an old church railing gate,
Feel the pain, see the blood
Running out like an autumn flood,
Then you'll know the struggle and strife
That beggars the day of a porcupine's wife.

FIRST LOVE

She sailed away in a sailing ship
Across the saline sea,
And never once did she come back
To visit me.

It was for her an enticing world
That had taken her away,
And I was just a flash in time
In her long day.

Twelve pennies made a shilling,
Twenty shillings made a pound,
And naïve it was of me to think
A farthing would come round.

Passive adolescent days
Made my shallow being,
Inadequately phased
For seeing –

That to her I never was, I never could,
I never did exist,
To her who in that schoolyard
Had me so transfixed.

MAN OF SUBSTANCE

By selling his business in rags and bones
He bought *en bloc* the stately home,
With all its staff and all its gear
Including three acres of fishing mere.

We'll turn the historic ruined folly
Into a doll's house for daughter Molly;
Don't James be surprised, you fool,
We're turning the study into a bathing pool.

To be a shooting range with huge potential
The tree-lined deer park has credentials;
But who is that, the silly ass?
'That,' said James 'is the looking glass!'

THE LIGHTHOUSE

I went upstairs to put the light on
And there I saw a plant with blight on.
I squirted it with paraffin oil
And set alight the surrounding soil.
This cured indeed the plant with blight on
But then there was no need to put the light on!

ADMINISTRATING ANGEL

The questioning angel said to me,
'Would you like to have some tea?'

Risking my neck to make good cheer
I said I'd have a can of beer,
Followed by a single malt
And bag of crisps with plenty salt.

She opened the gate and clanged the bell,
Said, 'You can't stay here, you must go to Hell!'

THE VENTILATION FAN

Like Uncle Ferdinand
The ventilation fan
Never seems to work,
Is old and quarrelsome
And makes a noise about nothing.

But unlike Ferdinand,
The ventilation fan
Can easily be replaced
By a quiet spanking new one
That works without complaint.

But no one could hatch a plan
To replace Uncle Ferdinand!

THE FLEDGLING

Weaving in and out and round
The forest trees with new delight
And a wild excitement all its own,
Like the bumblebee is at bluebell time.

Sensing for the first time
Establishment of identity,
Freedom to move in any direction
Under the vast attractiveness of the sky.

Sudden panic at being alone
In this huge new encirclement;
Crash landing with twisted wings
In a flurry of feathers and dead leaves.

Ever watchful, mother thrush
Creates a new disturbance,
Distracting the circling sparrowhawk,
Allowing her offspring to regain its pride.

DOUBTING CASTLE

If you wish to spread some cheer
Get to hell from out of here,
For this is the place of Ifs and Buts
And Mr and Mrs Misery Guts!

Nevertheless, should you wait
And chance your arm with your fate,
For who at all can know
Which way the four winds blow.

Perhaps now you are over the worst,
And you'll never again be cursed
With turnabouts and much worse
By the writer of this turgid verse.

THE UNIVERSE

As a human I ask
Whether somewhere there is a being
Who knows what the universe
Is meant to be about,
And what I am expected to contribute,
Or indeed, extract.

Are we right to assume
So-called supremacy and control
Over other living things,
Like grass and flowers and trees,
And worms and cats and dogs,
And birds and even mighty whales?

Is it just our personal ego
That assumes a supremacy
Of mind over the physical,
Promoting our expectations

Of immortality
Not granted to lesser beings?

Immortality or not,
The question still remains,
What is the universe about;
What meaningful purpose does it have,
And what part do humans play
In the order of things?

THE NEXT DAY

One would think it could never be;
The morning that came after
The day the world had ended:
It was indeed a fact,
For the world comprised a mini speck
In the composition of the universe.

And now peace came to the universe;
Life on Earth
As it had been known,
Beset with jealousy and pride
And individuality,
Was destined to self-destruction;
Life was an experiment too far.

THE LILY

As I was walking down Piccadilly
Clutching my jar of sweet piccalilli,
I saw in front, a lovely young filly,
So I swapped the jar for a single lily –

White and pure, just like her;
She had eyes like stars but so much brighter.
But when again I managed to sight her
She'd walked off with some other blighter.

Now standing there in busy Piccadilly
Holding outstretched my single lily,
I looked a fool and felt oh so silly,
So I swapped it back for my sweet piccalilli.

AMEN

Silence; not a whisper of sound.
Stillness; not a movement anywhere.
No scent, no feelings, no emotions.
Light and darkness disappeared,
Sky, sea and land,
Land, sea and sky vanquished
In the dying moments of the universe.

And in those dying moments
Time ceased to be.
Everything stopped without warning,
Presumably as it had begun,
No thought as to the before or after,
Absence of panic, or joy or regret,
No memorial, no foundation.

For did anything ever exist
Beyond the playful musings
Of the Creator?

THE VAGRANT'S LAMENT

He sees her pretty face each day
And prays that she will stop and say:
'With holes in your elbows and in your knees
I'd rather have you than all the sleaze
With phoney accents and loads of dosh,
Dressing loudly and acting posh.'
But now he feels as if he's been cruelly kicked,
For she gets in a car that's probably been nicked.

SMART RELIEF

The scene, the general aspect was
A sunny one;
The brook in which he paddled
A fast runny one;

But his intension was not
A fun one,
For there on his left foot
He had a bunion.

EVERLASTING VISION

When fishes fly high over the mountain top
And the scarecrow strolls down to the sea,
When water stops short of the fountain of love
And the dove represents peace no more;
Then, only then, will reconciliation blossom
Between man and the world that's about him.

THE GIRLS

Isobel
I knew quite well,
She came from France
One glance I fell.

She kissed me twice,
Just to entice
Me into church
To confetti and rice.

But I caught a cold
And none too bold,
Ran off home,
Heather, my wife to enfold.

She opened the door
I felt so secure,
But she shot me dead
For I was fully insured.

They honeymooned together,
Isobel and Heather,
Birds of a feather
An unbreakable tether.

But little did they know,
Lurking in the shadow,
My legitimate wife
Would steal the show.

A DREAM FROM A HOSPICE BED

On the stained glass window
Are the shadows from the trees outside
Wavering in the wind,
I see the angel float down
And join the shepherd and his flock
On the mountainside.

Then with no warning, the angel and the sheep
Ascend into Heaven
Leaving the shepherd alone,
Forlorn, desolate.
I back away; that shepherd is me,
So very much godforsaken, in an empty place.

WILD GEESE

Morning and evening they came from the east
At a measured speed, and at a height to avoid
The tallest trees and the pylon wires.
Flying in strict formation, wave after wave
Like enemy bombers during the blitz
Over London, Coventry or Liverpool.

To us on the ground we stop and stare
And feel reduced to the size of pigmies;
Garden birds are for the moment disregarded,
Seeming petty, quarrelsome, mean,
Even the solitary blackbird's song
Is hushed beneath the spectacle.

One would think we were being invaded
By some extraterrestrial machine
But for the varied individual squawks
Coming piercingly loud from the skein,
And the trailing stragglers, laggardly
Showing signs of their vulnerability.

IN THE NIGHT

In the night I heard the noise
Of voices shouting, laughing loud,
Carrying on with routine life
Giving no regard to light or dark.

I hear the noise of other things,
Creaking walls and water pipes
Contracting back to their normal shape
After a day of exceptional heat.

Outstandingly, I hear my mind
Checking over the past day's work
Then rehearsing for the coming day,
Those difficult encounters.

But deep inside I sense the sound
Of unheard whisperings of my vanity
Attempting to make an indelible mark
Upon the confusions of this transient life.

LIKES

I like to lick my fingers after a relaxed meal
If that meal is from a kerbside vending van,
And comprises a beef burger crammed in a bap
With oozing onion fries and sauce that's spicy.

I like to view the sunset on a late summer's night
Extending streaks of red and gold across the sky,
I sense the birds close by are also bewitched into silence
As together we anticipate the prospect of the warm night.

I like fanciful imaginary things,
To be with the smoke curling up from the fire,
To be a part of the snow as it melts into water
And readily absorbs without noise into the earth.

I like the dream when I fly through the air
And hover above an inaccessible place,
Like the sheer face of a high mountainside,
Precipitous, no one has climbed and no one will.

THE POND

Deep and mysterious, may it continue to be so;
Let it be the tranquil manifestation
Of things beyond immediate attainment,
Not like our food and drink, or the air we breathe,
The instant knowledge and communication
Through television and computer internet.

The progress to satisfaction in modern life
Is to just scratch the surface of seeking,
Better to hold, to own, to have,
To absorb the living of life into routine,
And to scratch again but taking care
To keep to the shallows, avoiding the depth.

The surface of the pond occasionally ripples,
Protecting its mystery for the time being.

FAITH

Can anyone reach the height
Where they can say
That they have spiritually arrived?

So far as I am concerned
An obstinate fundamental problem
Gets in the way.

And that problem is
That no one knows
Where the end-point lies.

Therein, the intrigue blooms.
Facts, knowledge, intelligence
Flatten into insignificance.

Suddenly, faith is the in-most word;
Defying all logic
It calmly fills those awkward corners.

Like drugs and alcohol
It softens and lulls the enquiring mind
Into acceptance.

And, in the end, is it in reality,
On any higher plane
Than the drunkard on the street?

POTATOES

In her vegetable garden Helen grew
Big potatoes for the friendly few,
Who marvelled at her bold endeavour.
They did not know, in inclement weather,
She bought them from a funny feller
Who stuffed them full of dynamite.
They had no inkling of their impending plight.
Nor did they did have the slightest fright
When putting them in the oven to roast,
The explosions were heard from coast to coast.
Alas her friends became a bygone species
When blown into small fragmented pieces.
Now Helen eats alone in her bachelor pad
And never goes out when the weather's bad.

THE WAY OF LIFE

The night frost came:
The damson blossom
Put up its shutters
Against the cold.

All in vain:
The glistening fist
Tightened its grip
As the full moon shone.

No noise,
No movement:
The blossomed branches
Surrendered their potential –

Sad but assured
That their vital core
Would revive again
For their continuance.

Like all living things
The tree has two sides,
The outer show
And the inner reserve.

WHEN YOU ARE GONE

No one about you will give a damn, when you are gone,
But they will squabble over your money, everyone.
From afar, a stranger will write that he can call soon
For the picture he loaned you that's in the living room
And pick up the French chiming clock he so admired
That you promised he could have when you expired.
Then neighbours each will beg a meaningful memento
That they will promptly sell, and fly off to Sorrento.

Yes, no one about you will give a damn
Except one, who quietly weeps and is trampled upon.

THE MONSTER FROM THE SEA

The monster from the sea rose up,
Crashed its head against the rocks
And exploded into silver fountains
Falling in flakes back into the waves.

The parents were not expecting this.
'Perhaps another day,' Father said
As Mother urged them back from the rails
And water cascaded onto the promenade.

As they had journeyed in the car
Their individual selves had transformed
Into a concentrated oneness of mind,
The pent-up release of excitement.

At last they would see the wide-open space
Of sea-washed, sun-dried golden sand.
A world all of their own to explore
With rock pools, sea shells, baby crabs.

The parents now standing and watching the sea
Combined embarrassment to their disappointment
At not having checked the time of the tide.
'We'll come again!' they explained.

The children found it hard not to sob,
Life was today and not tomorrow.
Then the monster rushed at them again,
Lashing upon the iron railings.

As it retreated back to the sea
They followed it cautiously to the rail
And saw it ready to rise up again;
Quickly they scrambled back to safety.

This they did time and time again,
Each time consecutively more exciting.
The heaving monster ever seething
And the children laughing, mocking.

'Come now,' Father called
From the open window of the car,
'There'll be many other days to visit
And play, making castles in the sand.'

'Sand castles! Kid's stuff!'
They muttered as they munched their sandwiches
And the car moved on towards home,
'Anyway, we've promised to meet the monster again.'

THE LILAC TREE

At the edge of the wood in springtime
The lilac tree filled its branches
With blossoms and with the sweet scent
That infused the surrounding trees.

When the inspecting woodsmen came
They saw the winter paralysis replaced
By the sap of life in the taller trees,
And the groaning silence by the song of birds.

And under the growing canopy
The brambles shot out their prickles of fire,
Competing with the bracken's opening furls.
Then they saw the lilac tree.

'Truly incongruous,' the woodsmen said,
Using their clipboards to scribble notes.
In that autumn workmen came, taking her away
To a more favoured spot in the municipal park.

She showed her resistance as best she could,
Understood only by the trees of the wood
But treated by these powerful men
As if they were dealing with a wayward child.

They pruned her wildness into a smooth shape,
Watered her roots into mixtures of loam and peat,
Set her in a bed of ornamental shrubs
Where she became the latest ornament.

She didn't flower the following spring
And the wood lay dormant beyond its time.
The wise men nodded and scribbled away,
Winter had been hard, they said.

They didn't understand;
They did not understand.

THE RIVER

Quickens its flow over boulders, twists and turns
And being fed by undisciplined tributaries
The river widens and deepens at the final bend
Before cascading over the bedrock to the plain below.

The thirty-foot fall had changed the whole concept
Of its relationship with the surrounding environment,
No more its joys and laughter, its sorrows and tears,
For at that moment the river had become of age.

Gone, the hide and seek amongst the rocks
And the languishing on sultry days in shallow pools,
Or burnishing tree roots to look like gnashing teeth
When storms are lashing and the torrent in full spate.

Now comes sophistication and sturdy restraint,
Wide, smooth, ambling, reflecting skies of blue,
Onwards, further down, commercial navigation
Plying from the trading cities to the open sea.

In human terms the river had gained adulthood,
Its tripping-up laces had been tied, its hair combed.
The babbling trickle of the high hills was gone,
It had become what it now was – a force to be dealt with.

CONVERSATION PIECE

Polly the purple pineapple sat at the table with Alice,
Awkward, unsure and sad, for she felt not a part of things.
'Whatever's the matter?' Alice asked, smoothing her party
frock.
'Well, look at me,' said Polly, quite put out at the question.
'I haven't the manners, or the talk, and just look at my
shape!'
'What's wrong with your shape?' Alice asked, looking her up
and down.
'You're a perfect pineapple shape, wonderful!'
'And my colour,' Polly persisted, only slightly mollified.
'Who's ever heard of a grown-up purple pineapple?'
Alice thought and twiddled her thumbs for a while, then
said,
'Purple stands for royalty, you are regal, a pineapple princess.'
At this Alice rang the bell for afternoon tea.

TOM

I think his sunset came too soon;
The flower beds he had loved so much,
The neat lawn, the high hawthorn hedge
Merged into a flat vague darkness.

I now stood where I had so often stood
Together with him, on the gravel path,

And sensed a short movement, a shift of air
In that still silent moonless night.

Perhaps this was his way of saying goodbye;
To him, leaving was not premature
And to glorify in his own creations
Was definitely not part of him.

Unlike me, who loved to delight
On the garden created from the wilderness;
The colours, the scent, the busying bees
And the blackbird at song in the apple tree.

Surely his uncomplicated genius
Will live on in another world,
Or, as a precious seed, lie dormant
Awaiting the time to be born again.

THE TREE

The wind is not blowing in the tree,
The tree is no longer there to see.
Despite the pleadings on my knee
They have taken the tree away from me.

The birds are not singing on the bough
For the tree can't be seen, no how!
There are no blossomed branches fair
For the blossom tree is no longer there.

THEY WOULDN'T UNDERSTAND

The little girl, as nurse, went to her doll
And gave her kiss-of-life resuscitation,
Lifted her gently and laid her in her cot,
Whispering words and softly singing.

As the doll opened her eyes and smiled,
A sense of achievement overwhelmed the girl,
A first feeling of being relied upon,
Of coping when needed in an emergency.

She kissed her baby goodnight and with a look
Long, lingering, proud and sad, she turned away;
The sun was sinking behind the copper beech
As she quietly closed the door and went downstairs.

The lounge was warm, her parents watching TV.
Her own thoughts swirled about her mind
But she would not share them with the grown-ups,
For, she told herself, they would not understand.

AT THE MEETING

Some said 'Yes'
And some said 'No'
Some woke up
And said 'hello.'

'What's all this about?'
They wanted to know,
Some equivocated,
'Yes' or maybe 'no'.
Some just smiled,
Their faces aglow.

The smell of food
Began to taunt,
Coming from the restaurant.
'Meeting closed,'
The chairman said.
'We'll meet again
A week next Wed,
Followed by
The four-course spread.'

MUSIC OF TIME

He danced to the music of time,
He danced to the music of time,
He danced all day, he danced all night,
He danced to the music of time alright,
He danced to the music of time.

Slave to the music of time,
Slave to the music of time,
He never ever missed the train
Even in fog or frost or rain,
For he was a slave to time.

Attuned to the music of time,
Attuned to the music of time,
He never had time to stop or pause,
Was never late for a meeting, of course,
For he was attuned to time.

Yet once to the music of time,
Yet once to the music of time,
He landed in an unstoppable whirl
Enticed by the scent of a beautiful girl,
Who outdanced his music of time.

She ridiculed his music of time,
She ridiculed his music of time,
She mocked, she cajoled, she faked and flattered,
Leaving his routine in shreds and tatters,
Destroying his music of time.

Now, alone in his ruins of time,
Now, alone in his ruins of time,
He recalls with anger those hugs and the kisses,
And on a late train home he fervently wishes
He'd danced to her music of time.

ABOUT NOTHING

There was nothing to see but the sea
But the sea was not there any more;
So he saw what he saw
Which was nothing at all,
For the sea was not there any more.

WHERE ARE ALL THE CHILDREN NOW?

Winter's day, nigh on noon,
The leaden sky glowers down upon itself
In the stubbleness of the waterlogged field
And turns its back onto the world.

The wood, despite its naked trees,
Hangs heavily laden, dark and dank.
As for the lone fox waiting to pounce
There is but a deadly silence.

Wood smoke from the parlour chimney
Drifts towards the village pond
Where mists thicken into fog,
And day turns swiftly into night.

No, no this cannot be:
Fast track the image to another day,
For where are there frosts and a clear blue sky
With the thrills and happiness of years gone by?

And where are the children, the snowballs, the snow,
And the ice on the lake where the skaters go;
And the robin, where is he espying food
And giving a chirp in the interlude?

For this day *is* Christmas Day.

THE DISAPPOINTMENT OF MICE

He threw it over the fence in disgust,
The piece of steak and kidney pudding.
They ate the pastry first with lust
But then there was nothing.

ELUSIVE TRUTH

Someone speaks, and in speaking whispers;
Someone sobs into a handkerchief;
Some people shuffle in pews admitting latecomers
And wanly smile in recognition.
The sun shines through the stained glass window.

Outside, other people go about their normal tasks;
Someone is trimming a privet hedge,
Another is choosing a birthday card in the post office;
The innkeeper checks his takings from the night before.
But here in the church all this seems strange, far away.

The tolling stops, the immediate silence broken,
The laden carriage wheeled to the altar steps;
Prevailing sense of death and hope of eternal life
Battle each other in that closed environment,
But in this world the winner would not be known.

ABANDONMENT

Pillows of willows at the end of the lake
Reflecting in the water like billowing clouds,
And nearer, a field with a five-bar gate
Far from the city crowds.

But she has returned to the city lights
And will never come back to me.
Oh, how I now hate this country life
And the things which were meant to be.

WISE GUY

Bright spark, bright spark
Come in from the dark,
And stand there in the light
So clear so bright,
And treat us folk,
Us ordinary folk,
As more than just a joke.

FLORA

Come, come forget-me-nots,
Forget me not this year;
Last time I missed the love-in-a-mist,
The flower I love so dear.
Busy Lizzies were in such a hurry
They hadn't time to come too near,
And lilies of the valley
Were shy and so demure.
So come, oh come forget-me-nots,
Forget me not this year.

A TASTY MORSEL

There's some nosh out there for me,
Loved and cherished and holds the key
To be wooed and cooed
And ravenously pursued,
Sausage, bacon and eggs for tea.

THE BIG SHOT

He had cursed the pheasant
That had flown away
From the stew pot
Yesterday.

'Never mind,'
He heard them say.
'It'll teach him a lesson
For today!'

BEFUDDLED

The atmosphere is thick with haze
As I gaze upon my beer mat,
Made worse only when the MP says,
'I want to make it clear that . . .'

SUMMERTIME

Summer came quick,
Aside the hesitant spring,
With bold assertion,
Like the seventeen-year-old
Striding into manhood.

Summer came quick,
Thrusting the roses into bloom
Before their time,
Like the young man encroaches upon
His elders' property.

Summer progressed,
Its early exuberance expanding
In its own success,
Like man begins to develop a footprint
In his wake.

Summer progressed,
New shoots bursting out of
The main stem;
Man with added confidence
Begets his child.

Summer continued,
Raising itself on high to survey
Its controlled domain,
Like man reaching out to review
His sphere of influence.

The summer continued,
Penetrating and piercing the reluctant
With an enveloping fragrance,
Like the man infiltrating his dominance
Into others.

Summer was fading,
No! No! The summer cannot die,

It can't;
The man labouring on
Feigns ignorance.

But the summer was fading,
Its final ring bursting out
Louder than before.
The man turns his back
On the approaching stranger.

Summer was now gone,
Dry autumn leaves begin to fall
In the chilled gale force wind;
The man puts on his overcoat
And walks away into oblivion.

FANTASY

One upon a time
(And this time has not yet come)
There will be a great light
That illuminates the whole of the earth.

Nowhere will escape,
Those thoughts which grow and thrive
In darkness and secrecy
Will wither, dying like birdsong at night.

It is the perceived wisdom
That family life provides bedrock
To human society;
This will be exposed to challenge.

The bright light reveals
The hypocrisy of family union,
The seething, the jealousies,
The utter waste of competition.

Once upon a time
Will come when individuals subjugate
Themselves to a common purpose
And combine their contribution.

How wishful our thinking!

LAP DOG

To where please tell me
And I will go,
Up towards Heaven
Or down below,
Searching the highways,
The byways, the paths,
Following the rivers
To the last,
And I will have
The satisfaction
Of having followed
Your direction.

THE TICKET COLLECTOR

Never a hair out of place,
The girl who passes through;
Hardly a moment to glimpse her face,
The girl who passes through;
Etched forever despite the haste,
The girl who passes through.

WISHFUL THINKING

The curtains are drawn,
The fire is lit,
The evening is mine
To do as I please.

Oh how I wish,
Being blind, it were true.
With the flick of some switch
My freedom was so easily come.

But then I recall
In the pitch of the night,
That when I was free
I had nothing to do.

CONSCIENCE

A single shadow crosses the moon,
Its reflection running across the field,
The copse and halfway up the hill,
Then vanishes as if it had never been,
Traceless in the annals of time.

Why then do these moving shadows
Of private thoughts, so idly voiced,
Return to haunt the quiet moments
Of my mind, filling every nook and niche
With fearsome, awesome solitude.

Those thoughts, nothing else but that,
Revolving, attacking, infiltrating;
A dominance suppressing all else,
Continually present, repeating, repeating
The burden of what should never have been.

Will the gentle moonlight ever again
Cascade as confetti over my forlorn being,
Its silver brightness penetrating my mind,
Easing my heart and my soul,
Chasing away the demon plague?

THE WAVE

In Southampton water amidst the roar
I saw a wave I had met before.
We reminisced about the past
And when we came to part at last,
We vowed to meet again one day
On the shore of Botany Bay.

PEOPLE

Pluck and put together grapes from the vine
And they will produce the finest of wine.
Put people together in a solitary room
And they will argue, and all too soon,
Produce the tattered remnants of a plan,
A compromise that never began.

PARTNERS

I wonder if you can see what I see
As we travel together on this fateful day
In silence along this long, deserted road.
I wonder if you can see the hedgerows
Rushing at us, seeming unable to stop,
Swerving and crashing, missing us by inches.

And on the horizon can you see the hills,
Pale and mysterious as the morning mists
Vaporise and disperse in the warmth of the sun?

And now, wild grass verges and fields give way
To parkland, specimen trees and asphalt drives
Leading to mansions discreetly out of sight.
Now there is traffic and houses with front gardens,
And houses without, with windows coming up to the
road,
The bustle and bewilderment of the town centre,
The noise, the flashing lights, the jostling of traffic;
The stifling futility of these things, do you sense it?

Forgive me, I am talking for the sake of talking,
Trying to ease the tension which grips me.
Since I lifted you gently into the car
Your paws have been on my thigh, and as I drive
I know your eyes are staring into my face
In faith, a faith and a trust that is absolute.
For a moment I feel as God must feel,
But I am not God, like you I have no powers.
I turn the car and we head back home together.

CHURCH

The solemn singer sang us songs
Decrying us for all our wrongs,
But as soon as he had gone away
The sun came out to let us play.

THIS

Let us think of other things,
Anything but this,
Of the dripping tap in the kitchen sink,
The towel on the loose towel rail,
The cutlery drawer that will not shut
Or the door that when opened squeaks.
Yes, think of other things like those,
Anything but this.

Or think of things outside,
Anything but this;
The blackfly on the broad beans
The blanket weed on the pond,
That packet of seeds in the garden shed
Which should have been sown in spring.
Let us think of anything else,
Anything but this.

Think of happenings abroad,
Of dreadful floods in Pakistan,
Volcanoes, earthquakes, rain-starved lands,
War in Afghanistan,
People against people,
Nature against itself.
Yes, think of all those things,
Anything but this.

Let us think of other things!
So easy it is to say,
But unlike the television set
We have no knobs to play,
Not even a switch for 'on' or 'off'
Our emotions to control;
We cannot obscure with other things
So dominant is *this*.

THE VIXEN

Light of foot, but nevertheless,
The snow came heavily in the night
And in the morning, pristine white
Evened out each rise and fall,
Each ugly scar from the winter's day.

The air was transparent, pure and fresh
Like water from a mountain spring,
All around there was a silent stillness
Bearing witness to the fall of snow
Having filtered out all impurities.

The vixen sniffed the self-same air
From the shelter under the brambles.
It had been a long night,
She was old and the raw open wound
Felt like a stab from a hot knife.

She had eaten snow to quench her thirst,
But instinct told her she must get food;
She licked the septic wound again,
Its fevered heat laying battle in vain
Against the cold, the blood congealed.

She found it impossible to move,
Everything about her was closing in
The frost-fresh air that had awakened her
Was now blocking her airway,
Choking her as she fought for breath.

She was unaware the heavy snow
Had invaded her makeshift retreat,
Conscious only of an enshrouding mist
Easing out the surroundings,
Anaesthetising both the hunger and the pain.

Slowly as the mist disappeared
She found herself where she belonged,
Deep in the forest where no one came.
It was spring, the birds sang
And she was part of a wonderful world.

DEBUT

Slowly from the darkest shadows she comes
Reluctant, apprehensive, shy like a naked body
Exposing itself for the first time to gloating eyes,
And like that naked body shields, temporarily shields
Its very private parts from the flashing lights.

Moments of panic, reluctant to move forward,
Retreating from the noise, finding comfort in shadows;
But blind compulsion repelled this basic instinct
And moved her into the clamour and the music,
The talk, the cheers, the clatter of tables and chairs.

At once the protective shield was torn away,
The naked feet caught the rhythm of the beat,
Sexuality surged through every limb,
Signalling the end of apprenticeship;
She flaunted her naked body before the crowd.

WHERE I AM NOW

When you have been
Where I have been
And love is only lust,
When you have seen
What I have seen
With gold as common as rust.

When you have heard
What I have heard
And there is none to trust,
When you have sensed
What I have sensed
That calamity is just.

Then you are now
Where I am now,
Above this vulgar dust.

SLEEP

Sleep is like mist rising from the fields;
Rising from the field on a summer's morning,
Escaping the regimen on earth
For the freedom of the skies,
Then assembling into clouds to provide rain
Which gently falls, refreshing the earth.

Sleep, deep, dreamless sleep
Where physical emotional knots untie,
Where time and place and circumstance,
After a while, become irrelevant,
Easing body and mind into freedom,
The freedom to repair, revive, reorientate.

Sleep is the mist, the rain, the succour,
The loosening of bounds,
The gentle loving whisper, the kiss,
The kindly deed, the hiatus.

PEACE AND GOODWILL

'Peace to the world and goodwill to all men',
A fine phrase, a good combination of words,
But is it ever likely to be more
Than an aspiration never to be fulfilled,
A sentimental utterance?

The natural world militates against this;
The elements clash against each other,
The warmth of spring encourages, the hail destroys,
Gentle rains awaken dormant seed,
Raging floods wash it all away.

Human families lie at the heart of society
And it is these self-same families
Which segregate people into competitive groups,
Contending customs, sects, religions, countries
Lead inevitably to jealousies, hatreds and wars.

Perhaps the sentiment is more farseeing,
To a time when earth and humans are separate:
A pure natural earth at peace with itself
And its human beings relegated from the earth
To their rightful place beneath some other sky.

OPEN BOOK

Let everything be straightforward
Like the four corners to a room,
Three sides to a triangle,
Simple answers to simple questions
Without equivocation.

Let everything be straightforward
Like cows in an open meadow,
A stream flowing clear and pure,

A stile through a thicket hedge
Into the woodland glade.

Let everything be straightforward
Like a full moon in the sky,
Like slippers warming in the hearth,
Like the smell of mint sauce spreading
Over freshly cooked lamb.

Let everything be straightforward
Like daytime follows night,
Like spring follows winter and summer is hot,
Like – I love you and you love me.
But everything is not.

BLIND POET

He wrote with frenzied inspiration
A masterpiece for the nation
But then he found
His ballpoint had unwound
And the page showed bare
With a poem that wasn't there.

THE COCKTAIL CABINET

They arrived in Bentleys and Rolls-Royces
To speak with strong dissenting voices,
But this motley of nitwits

Over sherry and biscuits,
Succumbed to the chairman's choices.

GUILT

It moved slowly
Like the shadows
Between tall buildings
On a bright day.

But unlike a shadow
It was not controlled
By the sun
Or shaped by a building.

It came from the hills
Of its own volition,
Determined, relentless,
Purposeful.

It was not distracted
By the Norman church
Or by the farm buildings
As it eased across the river.

The nearer it came,
Its heat deepened,
Setting fire
To token innocence.

Superficiality
Was engulfed, consumed
By its flame,
Destroying cowardly pretence.

The judge and jury Hell
Lay within,
The sentence
Was forever.

TEA MACHINE

Oh just my luck!
I had found a place to sup,
To slake my thirst.
The hot tea came first,
Then the empty cup.

THE BLACKBIRD

I sat alone on the patio
Listening to the blackbird's song
Competing with the constant drone
Of traffic on the motorway.

The sun rose high above the flats,
Deepening the hazy blueness of the sky,
Bringing, at last, a true summer's day
Crammed between the wind and the rain.

The patient blackbird continued to sing
As I continued to sit alone.
Slowly, as the minutes passed,
The distance between us began to shrink.

The barrier that separated our species
Had become unnatural
And momentarily we joined together
To celebrate our existence.

YOU CAN TAKE IT WITH YOU

For a man called Goldsmith
It is no surprise
That he is filthy rich
As his name implies.

So maybe it's not odd of him
That he should employ a boffin
To design deep pockets
In his coffin!

CAT'S-EYE VIEW

Despite
Electric light
I prefer
To purr
In firelight.

EVENING

Morning sped into afternoon
As if it were on the motorway,
But with evening, calm prevailed
And spread its attention laterally
To thoughts and happenings of the day.

Evenings, whatever the season,
Be it dark, cold, fog or ice,
But warmed by a fire and a glass of wine
Or sun-decked with bees and scent of flowers,
Are conducive to thoughts of the past or the morrow.

Evenings provide one with a measure,
A personal measure to pursue in reverie
Indelible flagships of accomplishments
Or failures that cannot be rewritten,
And fleeting glimpses of an unclear future.

OVERHEARD IN THE PUB

I am here
The time is now.
No concern
For before or after.
I have immediately
To cut the grass,

Trim the hedge,
Clean the car.

Another pint?
Yes please,
Can't resist
In such a heat.
But I insist
The next round
Is definitely
To be mine.

THE MALLARD

The ancient mallard lifted itself
Off the lake, brushed its wing tips
In the busy water, and found
A resting place in the reeds.

Evening came, and in the night
It died through overexhaustion,
Drowned in a momentary fainting fit,
Quietly, alone, unheralded.

Death itself was finite,
Happening in a familiar setting
With water lapping on the banks,
The breeze in the trees, the stars above.

After-death was forever,
No words of this world could possibly explain:

A bare corner in a bare room,
A room that never did exist.

THE THING

From Idaho to I don't know
I've searched these places high and low
And now I know not where to go.

I've looked so long with such concentration,
I've forgotten if it was a near relation,
A distant cousin, a friend, a glass of hock
That I so needed and have now forgot.

Perhaps if I journey to Arkansas
I'll find some logs that I can saw,
Maybe cutting wood is my aspiration
Then burning it, my true vocation.

MINDSCAPE

The light across the moor is sharp and clear,
Many-faceted like a new cut diamond
As it reflects the sun in all its moods
Progressing its way to the far horizon,
Tempting me to follow and search beyond.

But I will not stir from where I am,
The horizon and all that is beyond

Is the territory of my imagination,
Reality with all its plans and its deceits
Will not be allowed to interfere.

Thought has no regard for convention,
It is free to choose its own place and season
And its time, whether it be night or day,
And, not afforded in conventional travel,
Alter direction to satisfy a change of mind.

So, abruptly within the twinkling of an eye,
All baggage abandoned, the whole scene shifts
To soft dry sounds of ripening wheat
In summer, in Canada where men are sparse as trees
On the broad flat prairie lands.

Then Paris in springtime, Christmas in Oxford Street,
The multi-colours of New England's autumn leaves
And, back to summer, bronzed bodies packed in rows
On the warm sandy beaches of the Mediterranean,
Whilst across that sea, mighty Africa broods.

Kaleidoscope; frosted Swiss and Austrian Alps,
Outback Australia's parched hinterland,
India and China's awakening and potential dominance,
All these places rehearsed, stored into memory
For those long quiet times ahead.

WHAT IT TAKES

One word affirms,
Two words deny,
I wonder why.

WE ARE WHAT I AM

You are stupid
If you do not heed
What I have to say!
But stay:
Are we not all stupid,
Do we not all hear
But rarely listen?
Are we not full of our own opinions
And anxious that everyone
Should know of them?

We shout from house tops
Or from mountain peaks
And hear only our own words
Echoing, echoing in the valley.
We speak impressively
In serious argument and debate,
Again hearing only ourselves,
The rest being a babble of nonsense;

Our ball speeding towards the skittles
Is the only ball that counts.

'I told you what was needed',
We say as things turn out rosy;
'I warned you',
We say if things turn out sour.
'Totally unforeseeable', we say
If caught red-handed,
We could not expect rain
On the last day of the Test
Or the earthquake in Japan
Or the bankers' cupidity.

Like it or not
We live in a crowded world
Of individuals.
I am what I am
And the world revolves around me,
Together our objectives
Resolve as my objectives;
We live to promote me.
We all think of ourselves that way,
Unique and separate and important.

LEAD US NOT INTO TEMPTATION

In the clear and flowing water
Who should he see but the parson's daughter
Doing what she should never oughter.

He squeezed his eyes into a focused squint,
Visually recording every naked hint
Which she was displaying as if in print.

Imagine his poor and wretched state
When the only reward for his patient wait
Was a coquettish wave from the vicarage gate.

STING

Life is as it is – a pretence,
A selfish contradiction so intense;
It fills its ego, its every move,
With evidence to prove
Its true regard for other people,
But whilst so doing, trickles its treacle
Sweet and sticky, an attractive bed
In which to spin its spider's web.

PRESERVATION

It was a chill winter,
Behind the coal fire
We had a back boiler
With lots of surplus hot water,
So we froze some for later.

WAVES

There is a notion
In the ocean
That land breeds commotion.

GRAPES WITHIN THE GRASP

Shouldn't we try to be ourselves,
To live within our capabilities,
To be stimulated by our own environment
And not reach out to that beyond our grasp?

We climb the hill to reach the other side
Only to find another hill to climb,
We are tempted to turn the corner of the road
Only to find another corner ahead.

My father, in his wisdom, used to say
'Do what is right for family and friends,
Put coal on the fire and enjoy the benefits
And help others to do the same for themselves.'

The sky above has magic and has mysteries;
The sun, the moon, the stars, the rain and clouds,
It is the same sky here as that beyond the horizon,
Tempting though this may seem to be.

CHLOE

With ears like rashers of bacon
And a tongue like toad-in-the-hole,
A face as round as a water melon
And a nose like a sausage roll
And with a pork chop chin
I could with a glass of gin – no doubt –
Make a meal of you,
Just about!

BREATHLESS

In a room
As small as a tomb,
He woke up and read
He was dead.

KNOWLEDGE

Dig shallow and wide into the soil of knowledge
And you will find fragments of many things,
Dig narrow and deep into that self-same soil
And you will discover much about fewer things.

But if, like us, you do not dig at all but just listen,
What you glean from our more industrious friends

Is confusion, contradiction, intellectual bias,
All in keeping with the world in which we live.

REFLECTION

The song of the songbird is sad today,
Why is this so when only yesterday
It sang to the heavens and was full of play?
Perhaps it's me who feels sad today.

PSEUDO INTELLECTUAL

When the wind in situ flies so high
Over the pier and into the sky,
And I in my sheltered inglenook
Sleep or doze with an open book.

When busy trams go along the prom.,
To Blackpool, Cleveleys and beyond,
And I just stare out over the sea
Enjoying my own company.

When you are in the lounge at night
Playing bingo to your delight,
And I walk back to my single flat
Where all day I had comfortably sat –

Am I then missing some wisdom on high
By letting my world pass me by?

NOT REALLY

I was given a job,
Well, not really a job,
Something more posh,
An assignment.

It was not really given,
It was more a promise,
A promise with an understanding,
You know what I mean.

It was not so much a promise,
It was more a maybe hint of
Something round the corner
Coming soon.

Now I'm in a queue,
Queuing for the dole,
Well, not really the dole,
The Job Seekers Allowance.

SUNDAY INNOCENCE

Sloping field meets river's edge
Where cows munch alongside meadow birds
And dandelion seeds strike twelve o'clock
As summer breezes lightly blow and play.

Where frogspawn melts into tadpole shapes
And freshwater shrimps wave magic wands
In a clear stream on a sunlit day.

What more do people have to learn
In church today,
Sharing their sins of yesterday.
When God is with us, here and now?

MAN OF KNOWLEDGE

N. Cyclo
Peed 'ere.

IN MEMORY

Whatever today in the afternoon may bring
I donate to you.

But the precious leaf fall of this autumn morning
Is mine alone.

To praise, to mourn, to bury in timeless remembrance
The living past.

ESSAY INTO NOTHINGNESS

Nothing is nothing, is nothing;
It doesn't exist
It is not visible
Nor is it invisible,
For to be visible
It must, at least,
Be thought to exist.

Similarly, it cannot be heard
Or touched or sensed
In any way,
Nor can it move
Or stay still;
It is nothing
It has no identity.

Oftentimes the word is used
To emphasise something,
For instance it is said:
Nothing but emptiness,
Or nothing but silence,
This implies nothing means something
Which of itself is nonsense.

Why have such a word
When it has no meaning,
Giving it significance
Without it having status,

An importance without existence?
Or am I talking
Nothing but stupidity?

REVOLUTION

His feet standing firmly on the ground,
His mind intent on things about him,
He becomes a magnet
A miniature centre of gravity
Capturing all about him.

Aliens, like wasps in summertime
Assaulting overhanging rooftops
To busily weave and build their nests,
Invade his already crowded orbit,
Unbalancing the compliant residents.

The man, the evolutionary,
Still fixed firmly to the ground
Tends with patience these new intruders,
Cultivates interaction amongst them,
The rudiments of society.

But the aliens were impatient,
Evolution was not of their vocabulary,
They had sensed the milk and the honey,
And in their frenzied haste, demolished
The cows, the bees, the building blocks.

RAGE

Let the rage roar to its natural end,
Then, on the shoulder, a soothing touch
To restore normality.
But suffocate it at its height
And it may sink underground,
Simmering and seething until,
One day, exploding with volcanic fervour
Destroying all and everything.

MISSION IMPOSSIBLE

When life on Earth comes to an end,
Will it be in the daytime or in the night;
When the sun is cascading down
Glorifying in the aftermath,
Or when the far-off stars of night
Allow some quiet perspective
To an experiment that failed?

LOOKING BACK TO THE FUTURE

The mental block was gone
And I was able to write again;
Handwriting not easy to read

And meaning obscure,
But at least I was writing again.

It was as if Lady Good Fortune
Had lifted the latch and opened my door
Enabling me to readily walk
Amongst the lilac blossoms
And smell their scent again . . .

To sit at the edge of the pool
And feel the fresh air swirling
Above the surface of the water
Where fluorescent dragonflies hover,
Darting and twitching . . .

To have sunshine and the rain
Directly on my face and in my hair,
To ride my bicycle into a headwind
And to deeply inhale
Into my now rusty lungs . . .

And so to be set free, at ease,
Able to write my poetry
With scant regard for rule or rhyme,
Relying on unfettered memory
To inspire me – a real pleasure.

For, most of my time I am conscious
Of my tiny room, my disability strictures,
The mists of uncertainty encircling me
Through which I can recall fleeting
Experiences of the past.

BOSOM

Eyeful!
Don't stifle
The cream on the trifle.

THE TOLLING OF THE BELL

In the morning when it was bright and the sun was climbing,
He heard the sound of a single church bell tolling,
But this could never be! There was no church, no bell.
And beside all else was the sound of a murmuring crowd,
But there was no crowd, no mourning congregation!

In the afternoon when the sun emphasised the shadows
And the crows circled overhead, the sounds continued,
But the intervals between the tolls became descending steps,
Dark and dank, and the crowd's murmurings became intense,
Echoing, irritating and engulfing his reluctant ears.

But still it was not, it could not be; it was false.
The tolling of the bell, the murmuring of the crowd,
The slow descent down darkened steps into the unknown –

All false. So he of high esteem curbed his broodiness
To concentrate and work on his clients' neglected affairs.

In the evening drinking sundowners on the terrace
And with the sky promising a good tomorrow,
He wishes good health to his wife and gathered friends,
But deep inside his mind the church resolutely stands
With its single bell tolling, and the crowd still murmurs.

THE SYCAMORE

The sycamore grass and the sycamore tree
With sycamore sky above,
And with sycamore wings spreading over
The land that the squirrels love.

That sycamore tree where you and me,
Passing time at once forgot,
Together we were lost from hour to hour
The magic there begot.

The sycamore, the sycamore
Reaching into heaven,
Where time had thought it half-past three
When really t'was half-past seven.

POETRY

Dear reader,
Do not try too hard,
Do not chase the message,
Let it come to you
In sound, in rhythm, in rhyme.
The words literally translated
Are but the horse and cart,
A conveyance with which to bear,
The hopefully, rich reward.

Alternatively,
The words are merely a hook
On which to hang imagination;
Close your eyes and see
The sky, the far horizon,
Feel the warmth of the sunlit beach,
Hear the tide, the lapping waves.
Probe the mysteries of darkness
And discover a jewelled universe.

Dear reader,
Do not try too hard,
Do not chase understanding,
Let it come to you.
Always in nothing there is something,
Every silence delivers a sound.
The ripe red grape
Needs only the gentlest squeeze
To free the juice of a fine wine.

AT-RISK RHINO

No longer giving a toss to us
And more extinct than prosperous,
From winter right through till fall
They counted just seven in all,
The species – the Northern White Rhinoceros.

TOMORROW

In the twilight
Before the moon had forced its way,
There was a sadness
About the things offered during the day
That I had ignored . . .

The dawn chorus,
The golden carp playing hide and seek
Beneath the lily pads,
And in the sunlit early afternoon,
The butterflies.

I wistfully hope
That the coming dawn of a new day
Will help me attain the joy of
Those simple neglected treasures
That I disregarded today.

SIMPLE SONG

I feel your love
In every limb,
In every thought
As days begin.

I see it in the hills,
The trees,
As life fulfils
Its earthly needs.

I hear it when the wild wind skirts
Across the street,
And in the drive
The dead leaves leap.

I know it when your eyes catch mine
And see my love,
And then outshine
The stars above.

REDUNDANCY 2013

Reluctance to do more than sit
In a vacuum;
Drifting down and down
To the depths of idleness
Which hopelessness brings.

The mind – bland,
Geared down in demotivation
But hesitant to meet
The enormous gulf
Of endless time.

PERCEPTION

It is the truth – he says.
What! What is truth?
Fact – he says.
Fact! What is that?

The eye perceives –
The hearing hears –
The mind concludes –

Mine – yours – his – hers –
Same sight – same sounds –
Same truth!

Same?
Unique the mind,
Individual the conclusion.
Yours – the blue sky and sunshine,
Mine – the thunderstorms.

NAME DROP

Percy Vere, Gerry Attrick
And Felix stow away
With Harry's son Ford
At Joseph's Lock
In Peter's field.

OVERWHELMED

Beach; noise of rollers
Breaking
As the tide comes in,
But I do not hear.

Hills; attacked by clouds
In the wind's
Howling,
But I do not feel.

City streets; crowds push,
Lights flash,

Energy everywhere,
Yet no excitement.

Heart in tatters; dejected,
Mind incapable,
Unwilling to grasp
Rejection's finality.

COBBLES

Cobbled streets of Brussels,
Footpaths of granite
Slippery, shiny in the rain,
An hour by plane
From Manchester's back streets.

But when both were laid,
Were world's apart
By sea, by train;
The streets of Brussels,
The cobbled backs of home.

ILLUSION

Words that come easy
Flow like a shallow brook
Over hard rocks
Which are still there
When the waters dry.

HOSPITAL

Hospital ceiling –
To the old man dying
A stretched far horizon;
Neither of them speaking,
No need, a close bond exists.

Trams in Manchester's rainy streets;
Saturday nights in cinema seats;
Steam trains in draughty stations.
Speedway at Belle Vue;
Threats of curfew
In Great War's aggravation.

Back-to-back streets
Spreading incongruous to the feet.
Supremacy of the Catholic church
Guarding clean, white scrubbed step
Where they first met,
And first emotions stirred.

A fine family raised
Amid the haze
Of the 1920s unemployed.
Seems like yesterday
The children played
With secondhand toys.

Quiet resignation
As eyes show recognition:
Held-back tears
As life's last breath ebbs.
Death
Brings no fear.

In a close-by ward –
A cry, as a womb
Sheds its child.
Comes from the widow a knowing smile.

SONG

Give me the top of the hill
With the wind from the sea on my face,
And the rain clean from the clouds,
Knowing the sun's just up above.

Give me the top of the hill
With the town miniaturised below,
Factory blocks of matchbox size
And streets like pencil lines.

Give me the top of the hill
With valleys as distant folds,
And rivers like silver strands
Of wayward windblown hair.

Give me the top of the hill
Where I can spread my arms,

And standing alone, stretch
To embrace the world and the sky.

DEMOCRACY!

Democracy unites us to the world:
Frees us from freedom itself,
Creates compromise –
Better for the world.

No idle rich, no starving poor.
A mass conglomeration;
No place for innovation –
Better for the world.

No wars, no daggers drawn:
No threat or fears, no bomb atomic;
A slow unification –
Better for the world.

No categories of saints or sinners.
Blending mediocrities
From bumpkin to philosopher –
Better for the world.

Comfortable – safe – predictable world.

EXIT

My winter came suddenly
And held me firmly in its grip
Even before the brimful of autumn fruits
Had been properly sampled.

Outside now, winter has yielded to spring,
Yellow of daffodils everywhere.
Also, hyacinths and tulips show their colours
And buds are on the rambling rose.

In the clematis above the front door
The faithful blackbird remodels her nest
Whilst her yellow billed partner on the lawn
Has head cocked as if listening for worms.

All things seem to have renewed themselves.
But no, not everything!
The ancient oak in the corner of the hedge
Has at last given up hope.

Here indoors, the sequence of seasons has stopped.
The winter tightens about me,
I feel like the leaf crushed into dust,
Soon to enrich the soil for generations to come.

THAT, THAT NEVER WAS

Belligerent crowd,
Battered, bewildered, beaten
And,
Speaking its thoughts aloud,
Was suddenly silent;
Silent like the nail
Driven by hot air
Into a bag of cotton wool,
Negating its potential.

THE PASSING OF TIME

Does that moment come
When there is nothing
But the passing of time?
A time when even that,
Sensing its own futility,
Glides at a quickening pace
Towards the overhang?

I hear the wind whimpering
In the loft above
And remember it whitewashing the waves.
But now that I am confined
It does not come close to me,

Does not refresh my face or brush my hair,
It is no longer an integral part.

Nor are the other elements:
The rays of the sun on my skin,
The rain puddling underfoot,
The clarity of moon and stars,
The ploughed field, the green meadow,
The noise of crowds in the street or pub,
All still there but out of my reach.

With the moving into history
Of these cornerstones
No longer real, just a memory,
I need to ask myself the question:
Does that moment arrive
When there is nothing left
But the passing of time?

FARMER'S BOY

He took her in a field of corn
Nine months before the child was born;
Now it's May and he is far away
In the sunshine making hay.

DROUGHT

Rain, rain, rain,
For there's no doubt
That we are in
A long-felt drought.

But when it comes
There will be pain
As we watch it pour
Into the drain.

'Catch it, catch it!'
We shout to others,
But no one does
For no one bothers!

LYING IN WAIT

I wait and wait and wait,
But for what do I wait?
Nothing!
Oh, do not show surprise,
For we all do it,
Wait and wait and wait
For nothing!

Sometimes, it can be disguised
By routines of the day,
Like the postman's non-delivered mail
Or the phone calls that never come,
We have waited and waited
For nothing;
Isn't that just life?

BUTTERFLY TALK

Sitting prettily on the wall
Red Admirals spread their wings;
What indeed are humans for,
Rushing about despoiling things?

INFORMATION

It comes like darts from almost anywhere,
Pricking me into immediate action
If only to chuck it into the wastepaper bin,
But more often to file it away for future reference.
Sometimes it can dominate my whole consciousness,
Occasionally stirring my emotions into molten lava,
Changing my concept of life and way of living.

Still more and more of it comes; students need not stir
Beyond reach of their laptop or their mobile phone,
Scientists fear that their own technology
Will overtake them in its haste to be out there.

I question and ponder my own predicament;
When and how will my last message come
And with what elusive enlightenment?

MY LADY

She weathered the storm like a tall ship,
And with hardly a hair out of place
She came again into calmer waters
Better for the experience.

Back on land in her childhood village,
Her feet firmly fixed on the ground,
She saw with new light the trees in the wood,
The grass in the fields, the villagers.

The old familiar horizon was there,
And together with the river and the valley
All beheld a new perspective,
For she had grown up – my girl.

I SCREAM

Why protest, Aunt,
When the ice cream man
Stops his van
And gets out a cone
To give Cath a lick.

RIGHT

Occasionally some things happen just right:
Need no planning or encouragement,
Fill a space no one envisaged;
Naturally, no pomp or circumstance.

Like loving on the rug in front of the fire,
Like the book opening at the appropriate page,
A favourite melody filtering through a crowd,
Like a poem hovering in the mind.

Because they easily slip into normal living,
There are no peaks in memory,
But in the quiet of an evening sojourn
They overshadow the rigours of routine.

HEADACHE

The little men working inside my head
Had a meeting and then said
They would oil the wheels
To stop the squeals,
But the organ grinder took over instead.

BACHELOR

I wooed her in a field of hay,
I wooed her almost every day,
I wooed her till she married today,
And even after, we'll still play!

THE TOKEN – A SONG

Give me the pen,
Oh, give me the pen,
Give me the pen
And I will write you again.

The 25th of Jan., it was to start,
From then on we were never apart;
By Christmas I thought we'd be as one
But by August you had gone.

If you want to start anew,
Send me the token that is due.

Send me the pen,
Oh, send me the pen,
Send me the pen
And I will write again.

IS IT OR IS IT NOT?

Is it or is it not,
At last, the culmination
Of all aspiration;
The view from the highest hill,
The glitter of the richest jewel,
The access to the heart of the matter?

Is it or is it not,
When the grasp has slipped
Off the last and final straw,
Hope sinks to the depths of despair
Never to recover?

Neither of these seem likely,
For that which makes good judgement
Seems not to use the terms
Of human highs and lows,
But an intermediate understanding
That promotes the acceptable compromise.

CHRISTMAS DIALOGUE

'I can see
A star in the tree,'
He said to me.

‘You can see
A star in the tree?’
I said incredulously.

‘Yes, in the tree
A star I can see,’
He said obstinately.

‘A star in the tree,
It cannot be,’
I said tetchily.

‘Well look, you’ll see
A star in the tree,’
He said forcefully.

‘I’m too blind to see
Even the tree,’
I said aggressively.

‘Well use your mind to see
A star in the tree,’
He said helpfully.

So I tried to see
In my mind the tree
And star collectively.

‘So did you see
A star in the tree?’
He asked enquiringly.

'Yes, I did see
A star in the tree,'
I replied with glee.

And as I spoke
He disappeared.

ENGLISH SUMMER

It had hardly begun
When the kitchen sun
Flashed in the pan,
Started the fan
And then was gone.

NEVER EVER

I am eighty-six
Going on eighty-seven,
And I wish to high heaven
I were only twenty-seven.
But hold hard the pen,
I would not want
All that again.

IRISH STEW

A style of poem, the limerick,
Was put in a pot to simmer it,
But in the hot water
It didn't do what it oughter,
I've never known so dim a wit.

DECISION

The Scotsman left behind on the moon
Found that he had forgotten to bring a spoon
To stir his oatmeal porridge
And with this calamitous knowledge
Wished himself home in Dunoon.

LIKE THE CIDER APPLE TREE

You raise my hopes, you dash my hopes
Like the cider apple tree,
You raise me up, you knock me down
And, like the cider apple tree
You pass me through the in-betweens.

'Time to fell, time to burn the cider apple tree!'
I shouted at its haunting presence,

And as it burned its two sides merged,
Bright flame enlightened the darkness
As heat scorched the earth from which it sprang.

So, where does that leave me?

MIND OVER BODY

'Get up out of your invalid bed and walk,'
And you got up and walked.
And now you are walking, open the door to the outside,
And you opened the door to the outside
Where spring was emerging with new invigorating life;
The bursting into leaf,
The fresh air coming from the sky above
Along with the sweet song of birds.
But your sense of freedom is shadowed
And tempered by a look of puzzlement.

The questioning look was justly aimed
And just as genuine;
Why suffer as an invalid
When we are not ill,
Why experience all that physical pain
When we have no pain?
Why was it that we were so deceived,
Both of us, at the same time?
Why was the misery all-consuming
When it never was?
Meanwhile, 'get out into the sunshine'
And you got out into the sunshine.

LAST MOMENTS

His smile is bright like the window
In the sunny summer's afternoon,
His talk is carefree as the wind
Blowing across the open moor;
But this is make-believe!

For this is what his audience wants,
A frippery, a heightening of colour,
An exaggeration of poise and persuasion,
A concoction of analgesic;
And this is what he also craves.

For deep in the echelons of his mind
He has the fear of loneliness,
The naked desolation of failure
Unable to meet the ultimate test
With no protection, no reserves.

As the sun sinks in the sky
A roar from the nearby stadium
Breaks the threatening silence,
'One up for the lads', someone suggested,
All of them relaxed and smiled.

WAIT

Wait and the sun
Will surely come;
Maybe not today,
Perhaps with some delay,
Through wind and rain,
Misery and pain,
Fields of flood,
Bruises and blood.
Don't brashly push
Or heedlessly rush,
Just wait, and the sun
Will surely come.

THE GUNSHOT

The shot was short and sharp,
No echo, no reverberation,
No interruption of time
In that summer's day
With never a cloud
In the endless sky.

And in the wood where the noise
Would have been loudest,
There was no flurry of wings

As the birds rested before evensong
And the squirrels sunned themselves
In the tops of trees.

Gaps between leafed branches allowed
Sunlight to dance on the surface
Of the winding brook.
The fishermen, if asked later,
Would honestly not recall
Any unusual sound.

But somewhere there would be
Reason and consequence,
Fatal or frivolous, but now lost
For that passing moment
In the gloriously lazy afternoon,
Now quiet and slumbering.

FACT

Sometimes I win,
Sometimes I lose;
Sometimes I am lucid,
Sometimes confused.
Sometimes I mistake
Black for white
And foolishly mix up
Wrong from right.
But that is me

And maybe you too,
And probably other folk
That once I knew.

Oh, how difficult it is to see
Our vulnerability.

MY ENCLAVE

In the south and east
And way up north
Snow is falling,
Making travelling difficult.

Around the corner
People walk with collars up
And cars are moving gingerly
On the dual carriageway.

But here the sun is trapped
In my sheltered little enclave
And the daffodils
And crocuses are out.

I wonder whether in summer
The opposite is also true,
When I sit and sweat
And somehow can't get cool.

Whilst over there they relax
And sip beer outside the pub,

Open-necked shirts, open-topped cars
Enjoying the ease of sunny afternoons.

And further north and southwards
They have hills and dales,
Cathedral cities and historic places,
Seaside towns with golden sand.

But no, the warmth of my pensioner's flat,
The daffodils, the crocus,
Are, here and now, my everything;
The start, the middle and the end,

LIFE

Been! Seen! Done!
Is there any more?
Is life an episode
Or is it a continuum?
A growing conundrum!

COMEUPPANCE

This is not of fairies and light.
If you are nervous, suffer from fright,
From misdeeds and murder
Then read no further.

Winter night, cold and dark,
Somehow, suddenly I was awake;
An unexpected noise, perhaps.
I listened, all was quiet,
The sound only of silence.

A dream! It must be a dream.
But is this a believable thought?
However, I must try to get some sleep
Before my carer was due to arrive
To help prepare me for the day.

This time the sound was soft and firm,
It was not a dream or the wind outside,
Or the fridge clicking on, or creaking pipes.
Someone was moving about below
In the hallway, on the stairs.

I froze, my hands clutched the bedclothes
And seemed unable to free themselves.
My mind went back to that fateful day
When it had all been a mistake,
Right and wrong intertwined.

The footsteps on the landing
Now clear and definite, stopped.
The door handle turned and the door opened,
My heartbeats raced and loudly thumped,
And there was blankness.

THE LIGHT THAT MIGHT HAVE BEEN

This time the light was bright,
Brighter than it had been,
And I had glimpsed it
Many times before.

As I stood
It came towards me
Across the field
From the distant wood.

In my innocence
I was as if naked,
Unashamedly exposed
To its influence.

But it passed me by
Without a sign
Of recognition,
To somewhere beyond.

And I sank
Back into the crowd,
Back into the ranks
    Of ordinariness.

THE MESSAGE

At last, in this particular circumstance
The news is good news;
And now I can contemplate
Elusive thoughts of a peaceful night.

Sweet sleep glides slow but certain
Like a velvet curtain being drawn,
Like the incoming tide over summer sand,
Like a soft blanket coming down.

It comes not with thorns in its side
But caressingly, deep in cotton wool,
And far off, with rhythms and murmurings
Of music of breezes and rippling of water.

THE FOURTH DIMENSION

The eagle lifted from his viewpoint,
Soared hesitantly to the other side
Where the rock fall, only moments before
Had broken the silence of that peaceful day.
He was saddened but in no way surprised;
Saddened because it had been his forever home,
Not surprised for he had foreseen this
And moved his brood to the opposite crag.

The river and its tributaries gathered together into one,
Fell vertically over the last of the cliffs,
Plunging carelessly into the deep ravine.
The fall of rocks abruptly stops its flow
But only for a moment. Angrily impatient it heaves,
Thrusting aside and in between the rocks.
Then as before, pushes on towards the great lake
And, flowing further, through the flat lands to the sea.

It was Saturday, early morning, away from work.
He knew this was his favourite spot for fishing,
With long deep shadows and bright specks rippling
In the waters there, in the ragged valley below.
But horror, when he found the rock fall blocking his way.
Feather-bedded, needful and lacking initiative
In his comfortable welfare state, he froze,
Feeble and lost with no sense of alternatives.

The fourth dimension is a summary:
The eagle's anticipation and action to overcome.
The river's successful 'bull at a gate' approach.
The fisherman's complete helplessness
Which illustrates modern-day frailty.
The diminished initiative of the individual,
So obvious when it is thought about,
When we live in a spoon-fed democracy.

ESSAY INTO QUIETNESS

Quietness is a stretch of the mind
Which incorporates within itself
The sounds of peaceful living:
Children at play, friendly chatter,
Church bells ringing, blackbirds singing,
The rippling stream joyously dancing
Through reeds and over pebble stones.

Quietness, with these accompaniments,
Allows routine thought to break away
From its local bodily daily contacts:
Roaming and searching in far-off fields,
Moving on further and exploring
The wide world with boundless energy
Where time and space, no longer relevant,
Are relegated to the past.

Quietness, when stretched to the extreme,
Eliminates even the simplest sound
And this quietness becomes silence absolute,
Like stepping from the street into an empty church.
Thought stops wandering,
It stays and begins to concentrate;
Sometimes enforced, sometimes in panic,
Sometimes inspired from a commonplace.

At the other extreme, quietness abruptly vanishes:
Thought explodes into fragments

Scattering into different directions.
Sound becomes noise, chatter magnified
Into shouting, birdsong drowned;
Machinery, traffic, roars into life.
Whilst hopefully, somewhere, quietness waits
Preparing to emerge again refreshed.

DIALOGUE

'Fool!'
'Who?'
'You!'
'Me?'
'You!'
'Why?'

'Look!'
'At what?'
'Yourself!'
'Me?'
'Yes!'
'Oh!'

'Well?'
And there was silence.

RESTING PLACE

He moved across the field weightless
Like the sunbeams of early morning.
He had awakened from the deep sleep
That comes naturally after death.

He was invisible even to himself,
No shape, no substance, no identity.
At the field's edge he crossed the brook
Floating easily over the flow.

Ascending the bank where the sand martins nest
And over the willow felled by the winter wind,
Here hazel burgeons into full bloom
Promising clusters of nuts for the autumn.

Deeper in the wood where uneven ground fell
Then rose, leaving shallow indent hollows,
Captive dead leaves stir with a gentle rustle
Resting in a place where they had always been.

Here he stopped and all his essence dissolved
Spreading outwards, blending with the leaves,
Returning to where he had roamed alone
As a child, happy in this special place.